MW01631182
Red Bull

aguilar

SNOWY

WHERE'S SNOWY ...IN OAHU?

THE ADVENTURES OF SNOWY THE DOG FROM AFRICA

Photography : JAV

TITLE: "WHERE'S SNOWY...IN OAHU?"

Author: Paul Javier

Additonal text: Jennifer Ziemba

Cover photo : Tyson Quick

Book design by Paul Javier

First Edition

ISBN 9780615321011

Library of Congress Control Number 2009909282

Printed in Singapore by Craftprint

Ten years ago on the continent of Africa, in the country of Ghana, my friend Ziemba and I met a dog named Snowy. He was barely one year old, his fur was tangled, and he came at us barking ferociously. We gave Snowy some fish to eat, cut his scraggly hair, gave him a bath, and we soon became close friends. In 2000, Snowy came back with us to California, and in the spring of 2009 Snowy moved to Oahu in Hawaii, where he lives today, by the sea.

His wisdom, character, and love have affected everyone he's ever met. If given a chance to meet him, you may also find that to know Snowy is to love him.

This book is the first in a series of Snowy's adventures throughout the Hawaiian Islands. Snowy's been all over the world, and one of his favorite places is Hawaii. From the sands of the North Shore to the peaks of Diamond Head, find Snowy in each photo as he treks across the island of Oahu.

Follow

my

footprints

in

the

sand

and

let

the

adventure

begin. . .

I start the day
in my front yard on the
North Shore of Oahu
...Can you see me?

I live next to Sunset Beach. Kaena Point is in the background. I love the morning before the sun comes over the horizon. The sand feels cool on my paws.
Can you find me?

I love garage sales. I see a surfboard, a Hawaiian shirt, and a pair of boots. Can you see me?

ACE
Dole
PINEAPPLES

Can you find me sitting in a farm in Waialua, next to the long leaves of the banana trees. Behind me is Mount Ka'ala, the highest point on Oahu.

Can you find me taking a rest at the Mokuleia Polo fields. Today was the last polo game of the summer. I'm taking a break after so much dancing.

POLO
BEACH
BAR

Can you see me going for a walk near Waimea Bay? I am wagging my tail.

Can you find me? I just
found a perfect place to
rest in the shade and look
out on Waimea Bay.

Can you find me at
Sharks Cove? This is
one of my favorite places to
snorkel on the North Shore...

Can you find me now? I am on the east side of Oahu. There is Mokoli`i Island, also known as Chinaman`s Hat.

I found a nice cool place to rest. Can you find me at one of my favorite secret beaches on the North Shore.

Can you see me looking out on Waimea Bay and
Ka'ena Point. I think I will hike Diamond Head next.

Whew! That was a lot of stairs!
I'm getting closer to the top of
Diamond Head...

Zig zag, zig zag…I'm almost to the top…

Whoo hoo! I made it to the top! I can see Kapiolani Park and Waikiki Beach...Let's head down to the water. (PS - I think someone is taking my photo.)

SMOKIN
State of Hawaii
behind railing
safety and
erosion
Head

CANOE
LANDING

Now I'm back down at the beach, and the sun is shining. There's Diamond Head in the background. I see lots of swimmers, 2 boogie boards, a white surfboard, and a purple canoe. Can you see me?

Can you find me in Waikiki resting by the street vendors at the market?

TIONAL
T PLACE
ha!
SPACE AVAILABLE

After the sun goes down, I like to take a walk at nearby Kapiolani Park...

The sun has set on another perfect day in Oahu. Thanks for joining me on my adventures!

Aloha,
Snowy